GW01164609

My Two Angels

written by Abu Ameen

illustrated by Rose Qassam

© 2021 Hijrah Press

My Two Angels

All rights reserved. No part of this publication may be reproduced, stored in a retrieval system or transmitted in any form or by any means, electronic, mechanical, photocopying, recording or otherwise without the prior permission of the publisher or in accordance with the provisions of the Copyright, Designs and Patents Act 1988 or under the terms of any licence permitting limited copying issued by the Copyright Licensing Agency.

Published by: Hijrah Press

Written by: Abu Ameen (Mubeen Raza)

Illustrations by: Her Illustrative Mind

ISBN 978-1-914402-02-9

For the two lights of my life,
Ameen and Sakeenah

Allah created angels from light,
   They obey their Lord,
      and only do right.

They never sin, they can do no wrong,
They're pure and innocent, mighty and strong.

There are so many angels in the skies,
And on earth, hidden from our eyes.

How many exactly? We can't guess!
Allah and His Prophet ﷺ know best!

But wherever I go, I know truly,
That two special angels are with me.

One on my left, and one on my right,
With me throughout the day and night.

They're called Kirāman Kātibīn,
And their job is to write down our deeds.

They write down all the things we do,
The good things, and the bad things too.

The angel on the right writes good deeds,
Like being kind to those in need.

He writes rewards and blessings for me,
When I share, and care, and speak nicely.

He writes good deeds after I play,
When I clean up and tidy away.

Giving food and planting trees,
And respect for elders are more good deeds.

And before these good deeds that we do,
We must make intentions, sincere and true.

As our actions are based on what we intend,
And on intentions do our rewards depend.

We must love Allah and His Prophet ﷺ more,
Than everything in the world for sure.

More than mum and more than dad,
More than all the toys we have.

Because if we love Allah and his, Beloved Messenger ﷺ, then this...

...will be the key for all our deeds,
To be accepted and to succeed.

Now the other angel on the left,
His book is where bad deeds are kept.

Hitting, shouting, and being rude,
Breaking things and wasting food.

And saying things that are not true,
These are bad deeds that we mustn't do.

But even when we make a mistake,
If we are sorry and put things straight.

By making *tawbah* to Allah,
And saying from our heart
"*Astaghfirullah!*"

The bad is wiped from our record,
This is the kindness of our Lord.

And if your book is filled with good,

And you do everything a Muslim should...

You'll get your book in your right hand,
On the Day when we must stand...

...to face Judgement and answer for,
All the things we did before,

On that Day if you succeed,
And Allah shows mercy,
and He is pleased…

...Allah will give you Paradise,
Where you can have whatever you like!

Flying cars or fountains of sweets.

Fun and joy and... tasty treats!

There you can meet Sahabah, and…

…the Prophets of Allah – how grand!

So wherever you go, whatever you do,
Remember the angels who are with you.